TaeKwonDo - The Art of Kicking

The Illustrated Guide to the TAEGEUK forms
TAEGEUK 2
(TAEGEUK YI JANG)

By Jessica Mandel and Alex Man

Illustrated by Alex Man

Table of Contents

IV

Introduction

A general look at Taekwondo and the forms:

Taekwondo is a Korean traditional martial art which is now an Olympic sport. Taekwondo includes blocks, punches, hand attacks, kicks, and much more.

Taekwondo is composed of 5 basic elements:
- Self-defense (hoshinsul)
- Athletic fights (kyrougi)
- Breaking (kyopka)
- Working on basic techniques
- Forms (poomsae)

Forms / Poomsae are composed of blocks and attacks which the students practice. A form is a sequence of pre-arranged fight moves against a number of imaginary opponents.
By practicing forms, the Taekwondo practitioner develops:
- Speed
- Flow of movements
- Timing
- Power
- Good technical understanding of the techniques
- How to breathe correctly in Taekwondo
- Concentration

During advanced stages, it may be used as a sort of meditation via movement.

In the preliminary stages, one learns the movements and the directions in the form (poomsae) and knows the whole pattern by heart.

The second stage is done by going over the characteristics of each technique and over the flow of the movements in the form.

First Part - Forms / Poomsae:

Theory:

Basic principals in doing the Taegeuk forms:
1. While you are performing the forms, you must keep focused and do each technique with power and determination.
2. Each technique is to be done precisely and well.
3. All the forms start and finish at precisely the same spot.
4. You are to know each technique that is to be done and know its application. Additionally, you must know where each technique is aimed regarding height, direction, angle and know which part of the body is used in order to perform the attack or block.
5. You must always turn your head and look before you do a technique. As the form is an imaginary fight against a number of opponents, it is, therefore, logical to look before you do a technique of blocking or attacking.
6. Each technique (block, punch, strike, or kick) must be done with determination, precision, and power, yet the form as a whole must be done flowingly, a balance of power and calm. Therefore one must relax the body between movements.
7. You must keep your stability, especially with kicks and turns, otherwise the body tends to lose balance.
8. Kihap (yelling) – make sure you do the Kihap paired with the correct technique. The Kihap will take place while performing the technique and not prior to or after performing it.
9. Rhythm – forms have a basic rhythm which should not be too fast and allows you to do each technique with power and precision whilst paying attention to balance and correct breathing. In addition to the basic rhythm, there are parts which are done slower – again, paying strict attention to the breath, and some parts that are done faster – which are usually a combination of a number of techniques of blocking and attacking, for the emphasis on power and strength.

Advantages of learning and practicing the forms:
- It can be done anywhere. you do not need anything besides a flat area and some space.
- You can do it on your own – you do not need a partner.
- You do not need any special equipment.
- It is suitable for kids, adults, the elderly or when you are injured and should avoid Taekwondo fighting.
- It is suitable for those who are not interested in fighting.

The Process of Learning Forms:

The studying and learning of forms happen in a few stages.

The first stage is to learn the structure of the form – the pattern. The second stage, after you know the entire structure, start to work and fix each and every technique. The third stage (which may take place even before learning the form itself) is when you practice each individual technique over and over again until you do it the best you can. Of course, you must be sure that you understand and know the application of each technique. The final stage is when you review and practice the form over and over again while paying attention to the quality of each technique, the timing of breathing, the rhythm, the power and so on. This stage takes years!

Remember, practicing forms is a long process, built up on repetition and ongoing training that never ends. There is always room for improvement.

Breathing During Forms:

Breathing is a very important in general and during form practice in particular. Correct breathing allows you to maintain your energy for the duration of a fight, form practice, and adds power to each technique you do.

The majority of each form is performed at a steady pace, with the exception of a few slow and fast parts. We inhale in preparation for a technique and exhale as we execute it, be it a punch, hand attack, kick or block. We inhale through the nose and exhale through the mouth.

The Taegeuk Forms:

There are 8 forms which you learn before the black belt.

You start with the first form (Taegeuk Il Jang). And as you advance, the second and thus onwards according to your advancing level and student rank. Up to the 8th form (Taegeuk Pal Jang) which you learn before the promotion test to black belt. "Taegeuk" is the Korean name of the Yin Yang sign – "the supreme ultimate".

The Yin Yang is a definition which belongs to the ancient Asian philosophy,

Two opposing but complementary forces that can be found in all things in the universe.

Yin – is the cold, shaded, materialistic and receiving part.

Yang – is the warm, lit, energetic and giving part.

Yin Yang can be represented in many different ways, another way is:

A straight line represents Yang 

A broken line represents Yin

<u>**The Trigrams:**</u>

A combination of 3 Yin Yangs together is called a trigram.
There are 8 trigrams.
Each trigram shows a process or an element in nature.
Each Taegeuk form represents 1 of the 8 trigrams.

<u>Form number</u>	<u>Nature</u>	<u>Trigram name</u>	Trigram	<u>Represents</u>
Taegeuk number 1 (Taegeuk Il Jang)	Heaven and Light	Keon		Creation
Taegeuk number 2 (Taegeuk Yi Jang)	Lake	Tae		Joyfulness
Taegeuk number 3 (Taegeuk Sam Jang)	Fire and Sun	Ri		Warmth, enthusiasm, hope
Taegeuk number 4 (Taegeuk Sa Jang)	Thunder and Lightning	Jin		Bravery
Taegeuk number 5 (Taegeuk Oh Jang)	Wind	Seon		Humble state of mind
Taegeuk number 6 (Taegeuk Yuk Jang)	Water	Gam		Confidence
Taegeuk number 7 (Taegeuk Chil Jang)	Mountain	Gan		"Top Stop" know when to stop
Taegeuk number 8 (Taegeuk Pal Jang)	Earth	Gon		Receptive

<u>**Additional Information:**</u>

Each and every form starts with a ready stance (chonbi) and finishes with a ready stance precisely at the same place where you started.
In many Taekwondo schools there are a few steps prior to starting practicing:
• Standing in an attention stance (charyot).
• Bowing (kyongre).
• Declaring the name of the form, then moving to the ready stance (chonbi) and starting the form.
• At the end of the form, moving to attention stance (charyot) and bowing again.

In this book, we give the general principles which will apply to all Taekwondo students. With this in mind, each Taekwondo school has its own rules and regulations and pays closer attention to different principles. Thus there will be differences in approach between different schools.
Also, there may be disparities between our book to what is taught in your school. Our book comes to assist and give a comprehensive review of the forms but in no way is to replace the knowledge which is provided to you by your instructor.
Respect your instructor, be attentive, and absorb as much knowledge as possible.

Terms and meanings in Korean:
In different sources, we can find the Taekwondo terminology spelled in different variations since it's translated from Korean.
For example the term "ready stance" appears in a lot of variations:
Joon Bi
Junbi
Chonbi
Chunbi
Chunbi sogi / seogi / sugi
Thus, in the book, we tried to always make the correct choice to the best of our knowledge and understanding when we wrote the techniques' name in Korean.

In some Taekwondo schools, the back hand punch and the front hand punch terms are opposite. Sometimes they are called "bandai jireugi" and sometimes they are called "baro jireugi". In this book, we call the back hand punch a reverse punch (baro jireugi), and the front hand punch a punch (bandai jireugi).

Taegeuk Form 2
(Taegeuk Yi Jang)

TAEGEUK YI JANG (2)

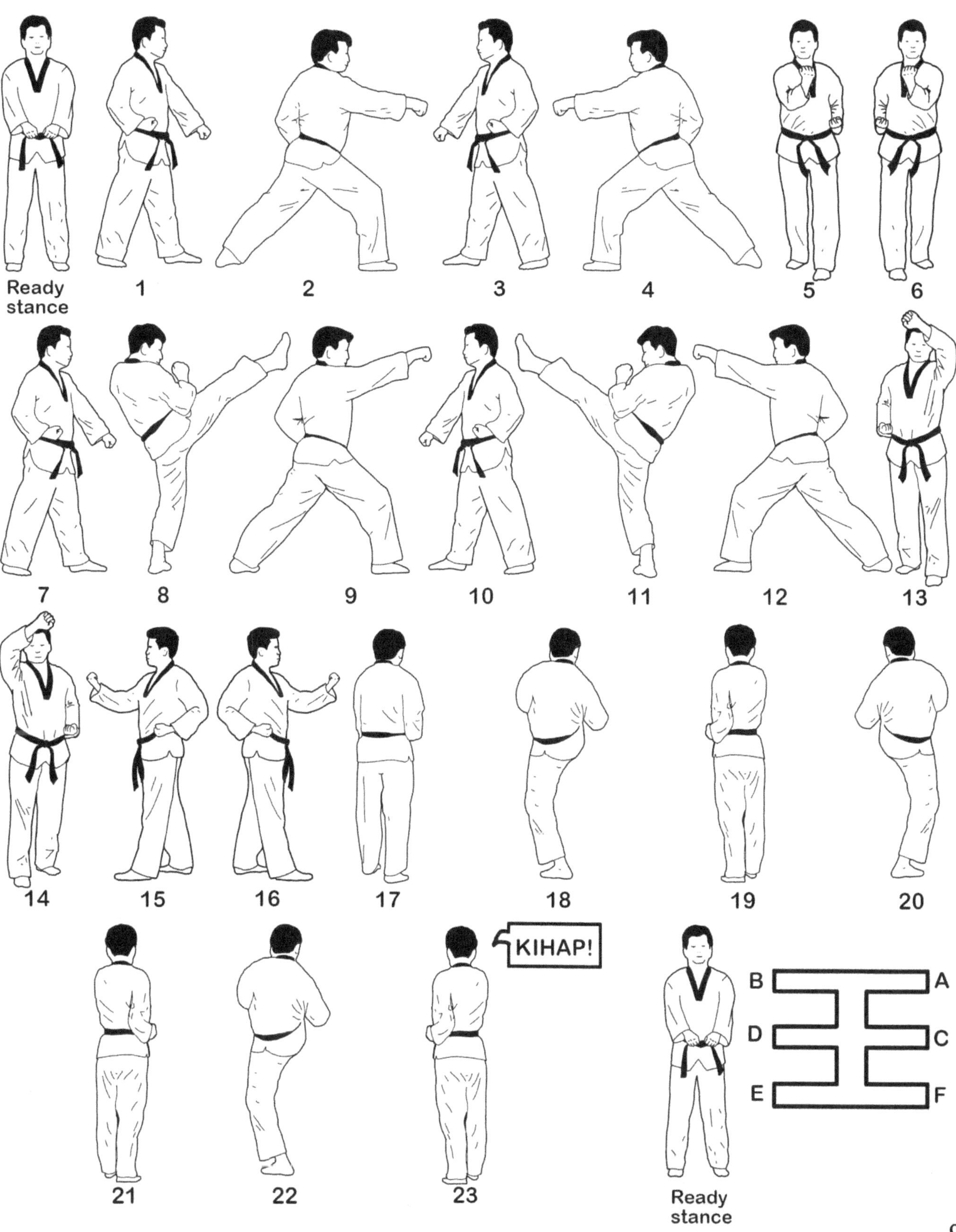

Ready stance

1

2

3

4

5

6

7

8

9

10

11

12

13

14

15

16

17

18

19

20

21

22

23

Ready stance

TAEGEUK YI JANG (2)

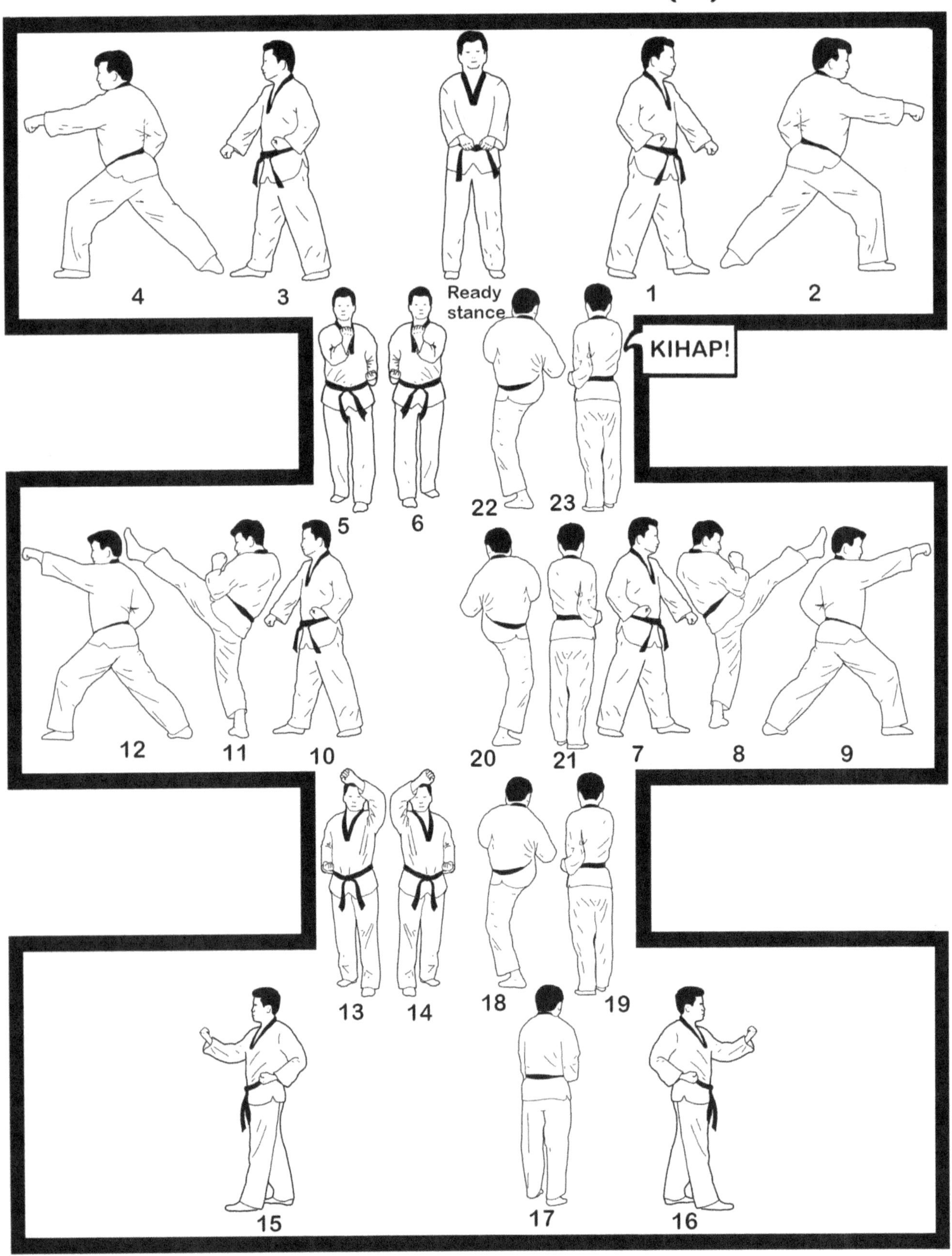

TAEGEUK YI JANG (2) PART ONE

1. Ready stance

2. Walking stance, low block

3. Front stance, middle punch

4. Walking stance, low block

5. Front stance, middle punch

6. Walking stance, reverse middle block

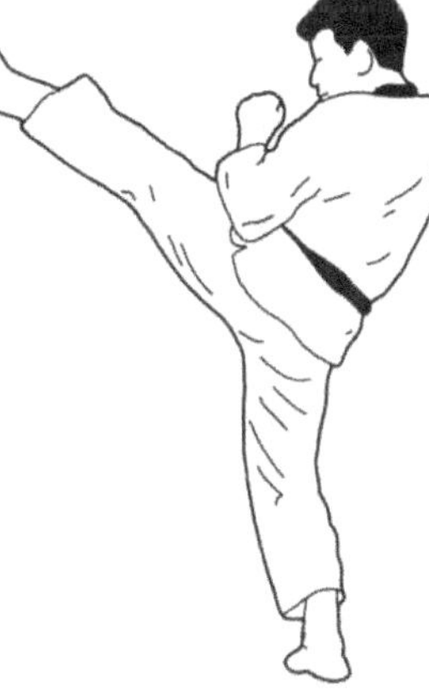

7. Walking stance, reverse middle block

8. Walking stance, low block

9. Front kick

10. Front stance, high punch

11. Walking stance, low block

12. Front kick

13. Front stance, high punch

14. Walking stance, high block

15. Walking stance, high block

TAEGEUK YI JANG (2) PART TWO

16. Walking stance, reverse middle block

17. Walking stance, reverse middle block

18. Walking stance, low block (Back view)

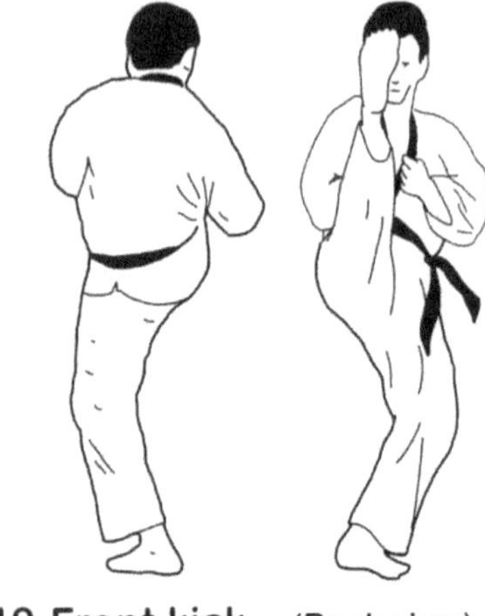

19. Front kick (Back view)

20. Walking (Back view) stance, middle punch

21. Front kick (Back view)

22. Walking (Back view) stance, middle punch

23. Front kick (Back view)

24. Walking (Back view) stance, middle punch

25. Ready stance

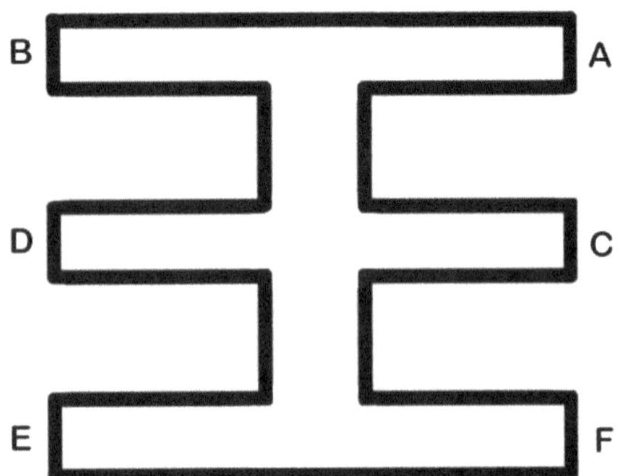

12

TAEGEUK YI JANG (2)

Philosophical symbol is - Tae - meaning joyfulness.

Regarding nature – a lake.

This poomsae is basic and is suitable for orange belts, geup 7 and up.

Basic stances – walking stance and front stance.

Basic blocks – low, center and high block.

Basic attacks – central punch and high punch.

1. 

Ready stance (chonbi) legs parallel, hip width (naranhi sugi).

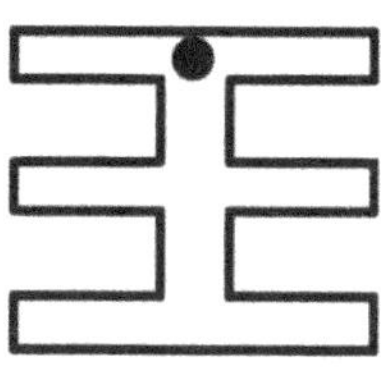

2. 

To your left - walking stance (apsugi), low block (arehmakki). Keep the block about a fist above the leg.

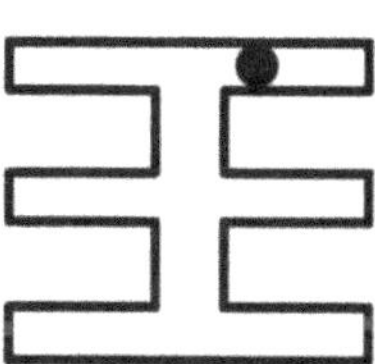

3. 

Front stance (apkubi), middle punch (momtong bandai jireugi). Keep the punch aimed at the solar plexus.

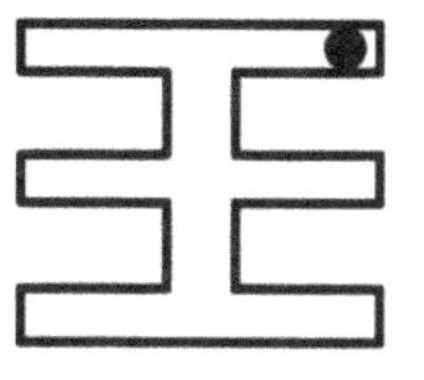

4.

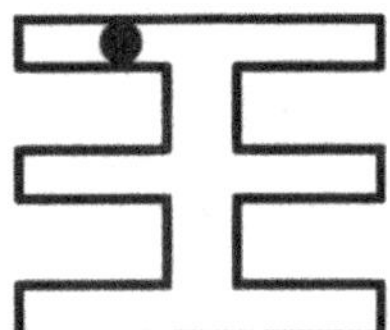

To your right - walking stance (apsugi), low block (arehmakki). Keep the block about a fist above the leg.

5.

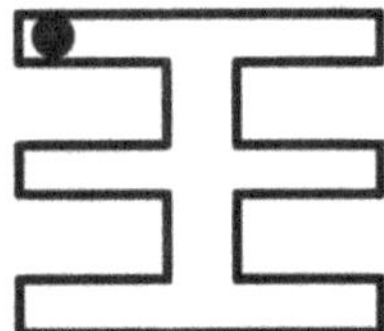

Front stance (apkubi), middle punch (momtong bandai jireugi). Keep the punch aimed at the solar plexus.

6.

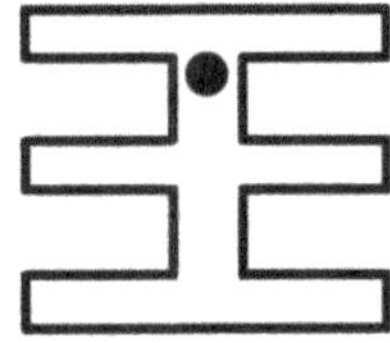

Forward - walking stance (apsugi), reverse middle block (momtong an makki).

7.

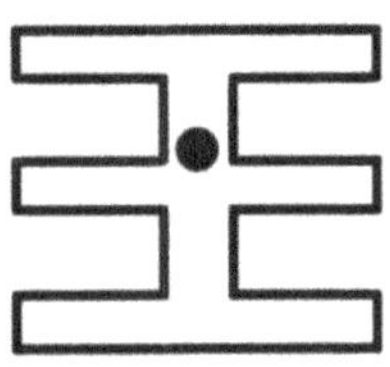

Forward - walking stance (apsugi), reverse middle block (momtong an makki).

8.

To your left - walking stance (apsugi), low block (arehmakki). Keep the block about a fist above the leg.

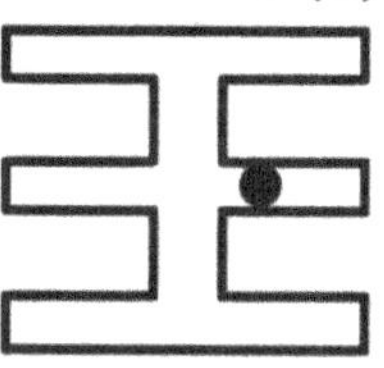

9.

Front kick (apchuck ap chagi).

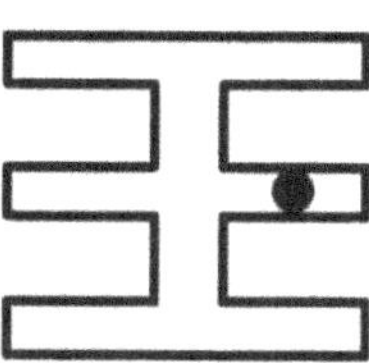

10

Front stance (apkubi),

high punch (ulgul bandai jireugi).

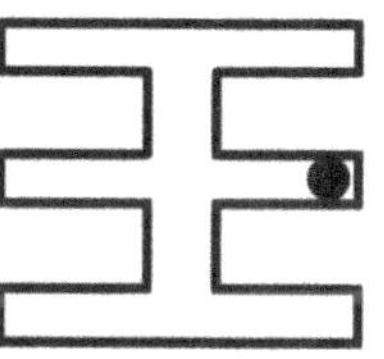

11

To your right - walking stance (apsugi), low block (arehmakki). Keep the block about a fist above the leg.

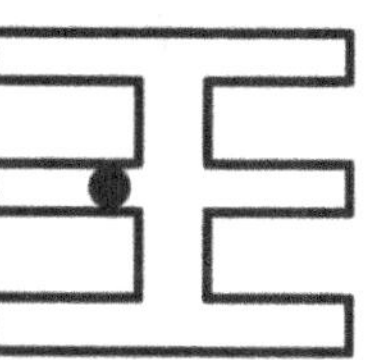

12. Front kick (apchuck ap chagi).

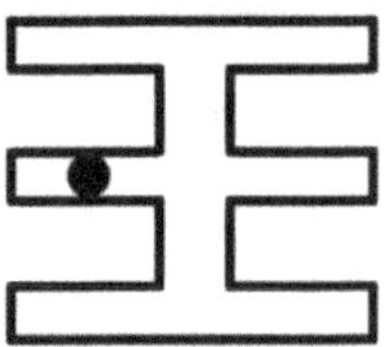

13. Front stance (apkubi),

high punch (ulgul bandai jireugi).

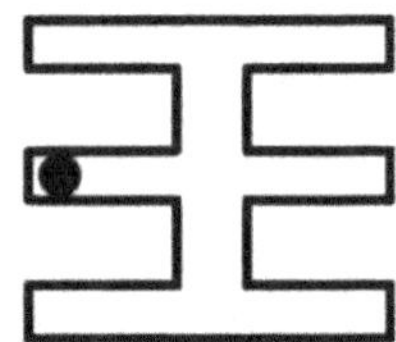

14. Forward -

walking stance (apsugi),

high block (ulgul makki).

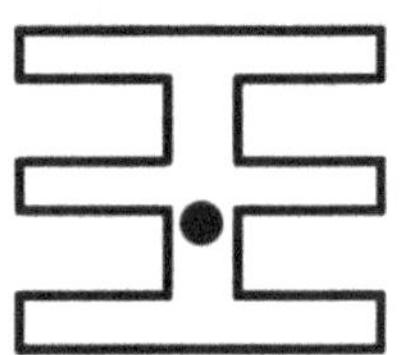

15. Forward -

walking stance (apsugi),

high block (ulgul makki).

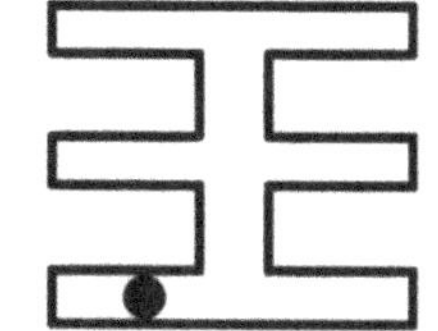

16 (Turn via left shoulder 270 degrees).

Walking stance (apsugi)

reverse middle block

(momtong an makki).

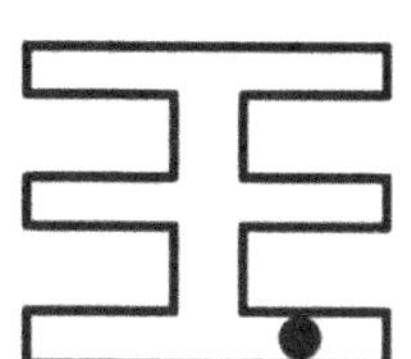

17 (Turn via left shoulder 180 degrees).

Walking stance (apsugi)

reverse middle block

(momtong an makki).

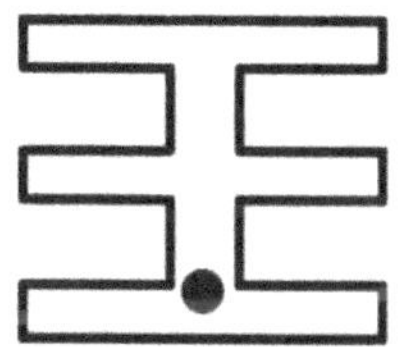

18 Backwards -

(towards starting position)

walking stance (apsugi)

low block (areh makki).

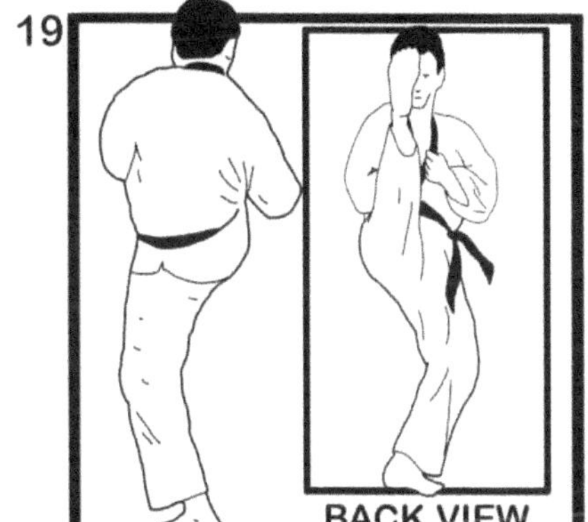

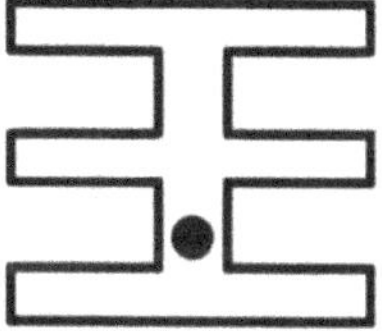

19 Front kick (apchuck ap chagi).

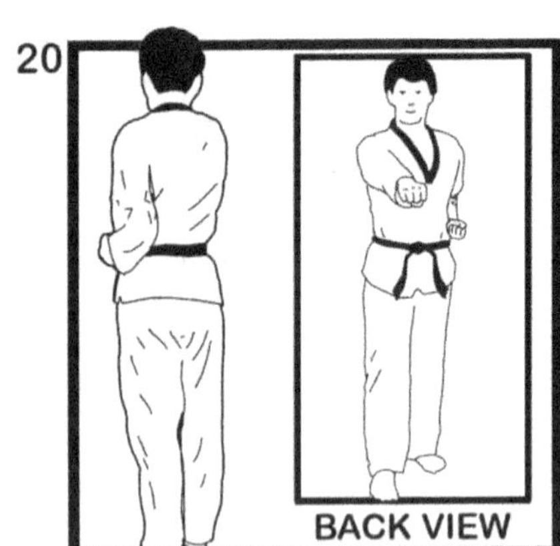

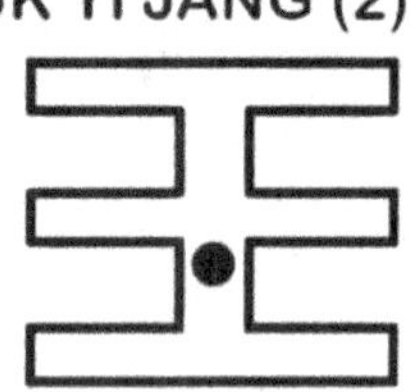

Walking stance (apsugi),

middle punch

(momtong bandai jireugi).

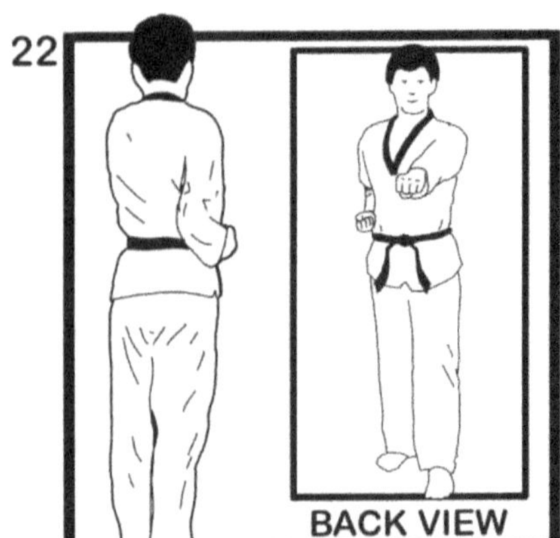

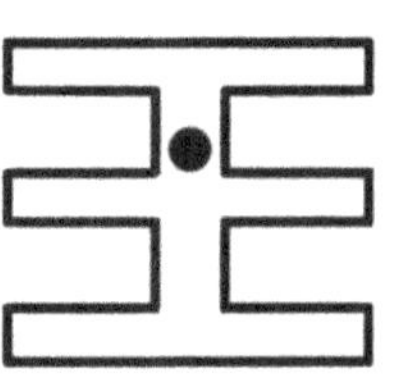

Front kick (apchuck ap chagi).

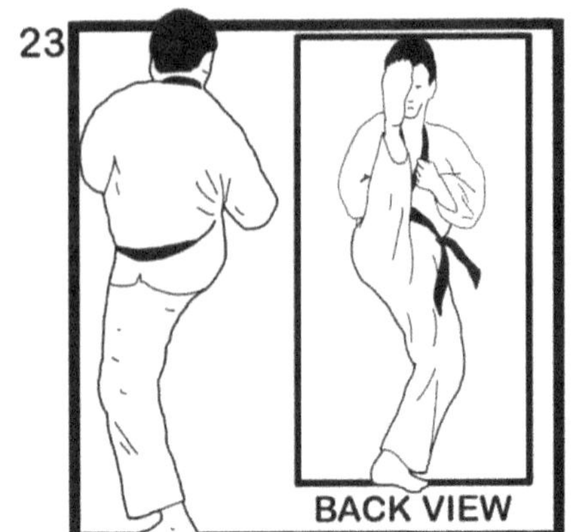

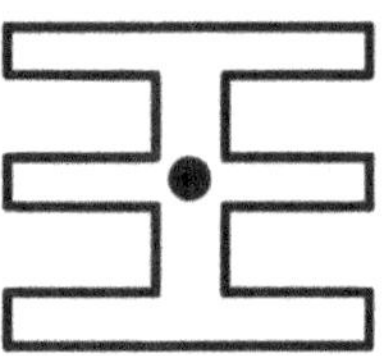

Walking stance (apsugi),

middle punch

(momtong bandai jireugi).

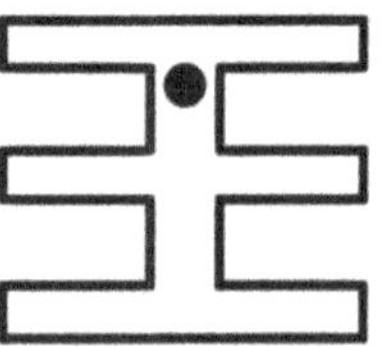

Front kick (apchuck ap chagi).

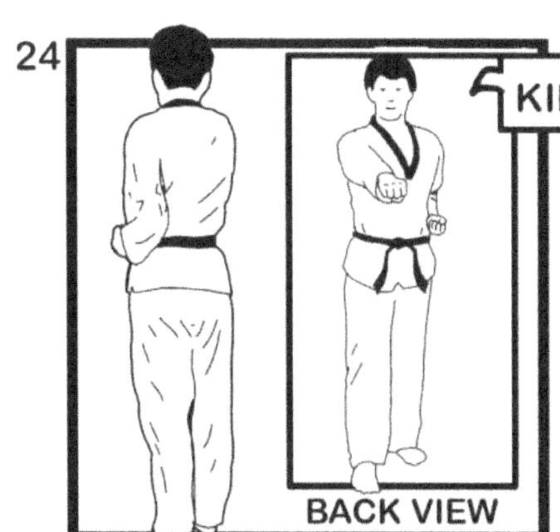

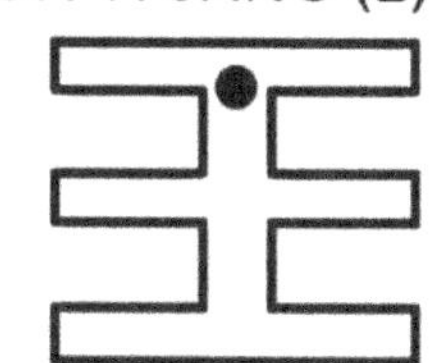

Walking stance (apsugi), middle punch (momtong bandai jireugi). Yell!

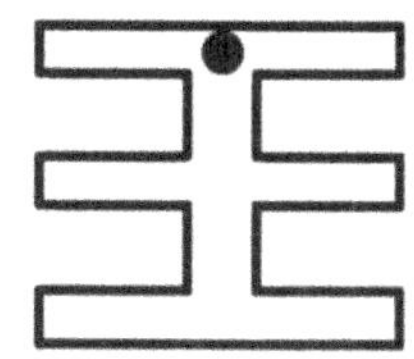

Turn your left foot to ready stance (chonbi) legs parallel, hip width (naranhi sugi).

<u>Second Part – Techniques and More:</u>

<u>Basic explanations for executing Taekwondo techniques:</u>

• Most of the kicks start with a bent knee.

• When you do a block, pay attention that the elbow does not go out of the body-line.

• When you prepare to perform a technique, inhale.

• When you perform it, exhale.

• When you do a stance, pay attention that your back is straight and perpendicular to the floor.

• When you do a technique, block/kick/attack, you have to know which part of the body should hit the target (ball of the foot, heel, knuckles, etc).

• When you attack, focus and aim to hit the precise target.

• The part that generates the power in Taekwondo is the hip. pay attention to always move the hip while doing blocks and attacks.

In the following pages, you will find applications of Taegeuk 2, and an illustrated dictionary for basic techniques.

Taegeuk 2 applications

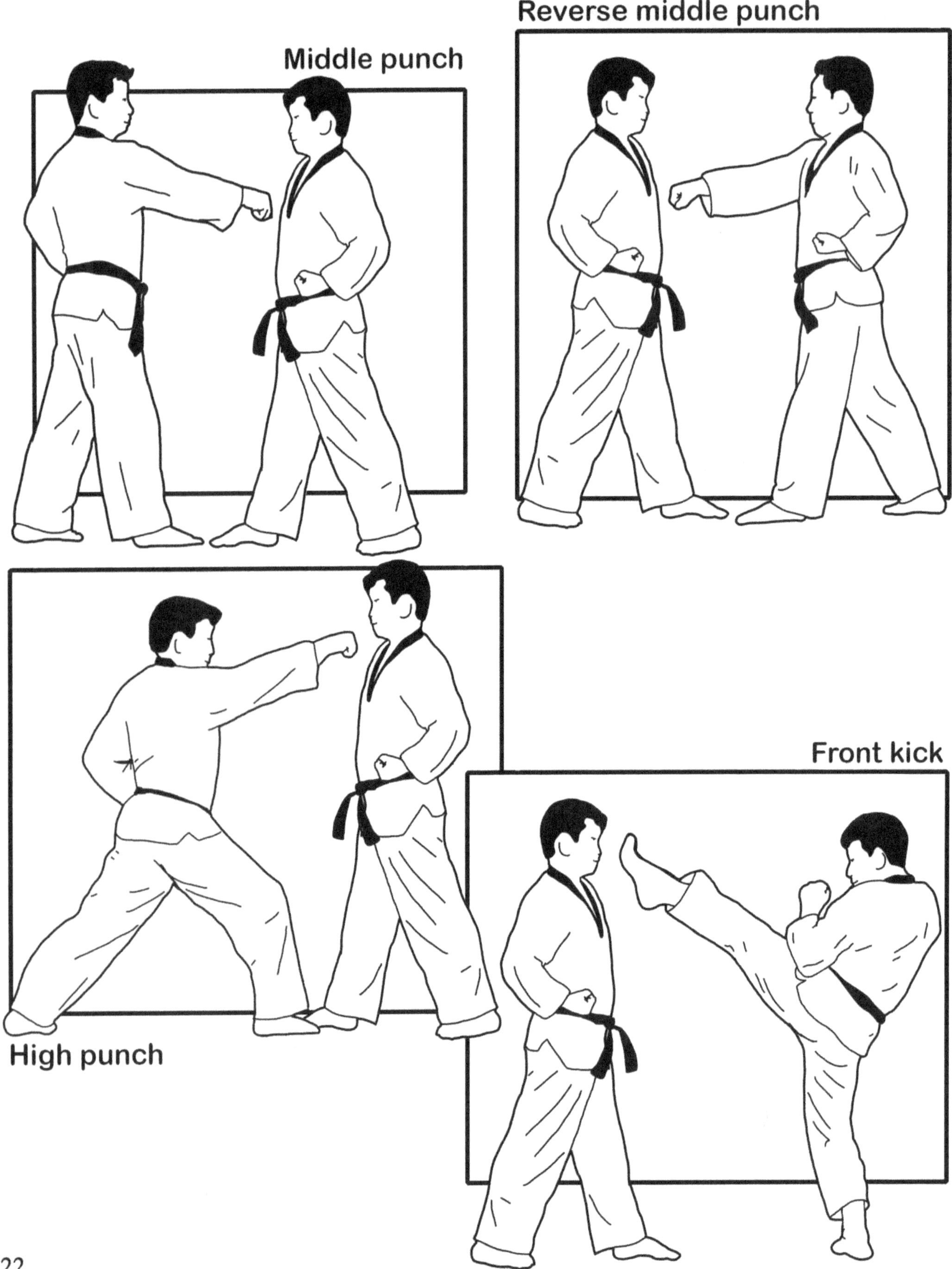

Middle punch
Reverse middle punch
High punch
Front kick

23

Walking stance
(ap seogi),
front hand middle punch
(momtong bandae jireugi)
PUNCHES
Front stance
(ap kubi),
front hand middle punch
(momtong bandae jireugi)
Front stance
(ap kubi),
front hand high punch
(olgul bandae jireugi)

Walking stance
(ap seogi),
reverse middle punch
(momtong baro jireugi)

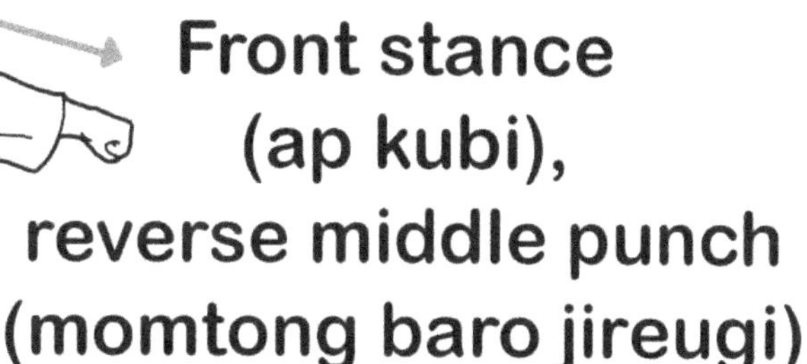

PUNCHES

Front stance
(ap kubi),
reverse middle punch
(momtong baro jireugi)

Front stance
(ap kubi),
reverse high punch
(olgul baro jireugi)

Walking stance (ap seogi),
low block (areh makki)
BLOCKS
Front stance (ap kubi),
low block (areh makki)
Horse-riding stance
(juchum seogi),
side low block
(yop areh makki)

Inner wrist middle section
outward block
(an palmok
momtong bakkat
makki)

BLOCKS

Middle outward
block
(bakkat palmok
momtong bakkat
makki)

Middle block
from outside in
(momtong an makki)

High block
(olgul makki)

BLOCKS

High outward
block
(bakkat palmok
olgul bakkat
makki)

Back stance
(dwit kubi seogi)
BASIC STANCES
Walking stance
(ap seogi)
Front stance
(ap kubi seogi)

Left Stance

(wen seogi)

Right Stance

(oreun seogi)

BASIC STANCES

Fighting stance

(kyorugi seogi)

Ready stance

(chonbi)

legs parallel,

hip width

(naranhi seogi)

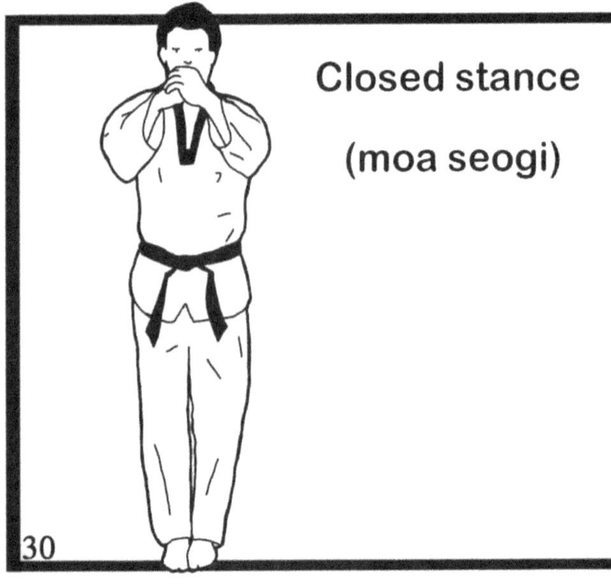

Closed stance

(moa seogi)

Horse-riding stance

(juchum seogi)

<u>**About the Authors:**</u>

MASTER JESSICA MANDEL is an International Master Instructor in TaeKwonDo and holder of a 6th degree DAN black belt certified by the Kukkiwon (Korea).
She has trained in TaeKwonDo for more than 38 years, has 30 years of teaching experience, and currently runs two full time gyms which attract an international body of students.
She is also a certified International Referee in poomsae (WT/ETU), has both competed and judged World and European competitions and is an International Referee in fighting.
In recognition to her contributions to the martial arts, the TaeKwonDo Hall of Fame recognized and honored Master Mandel as "Outstanding TaeKwonDo Instructor of Israel."
Author and illustrator of the "Taekwondo the art of kicking" book series.

MASTER ALEX MAN is an International Master Instructor in TaeKwonDo and holder of a 5th degree DAN black belt certified by the Kukkiwon (Korea).
He has trained in martial arts for over 30 years and has taught Taekwondo for over 25 years.
For the last few years, he also practiced the Moo Duk Kwan Taekwondo.
Always a student, eager to learn the fascinating ways of the martial arts.
In addition, he is an illustrator and an author of children's books. This book is a great opportunity to combine those two passion for martial art and illustration.
Author and illustrator of the "Taekwondo the art of kicking" book series.
He learned and taught Alternative Medicine (including Chinese medicine, Chinese acupuncture, and Korean acupuncture) for many years.
And most importantly, he's happily married and has 5 wonderful kids.

Dear reader,

Thank you so much for purchasing our book.

We hope you enjoyed it and learned from it.

We would greatly appreciate it if you could leave a review

of our book on AMAZON.

Hoping to see you soon,

Enjoy practicing Taekwondo!